Deer Diaries:
The Seasons at Cat Crossing Farm

poems by

Judith Stanton

Finishing Line Press
Georgetown, Kentucky

Deer Diaries:
The Seasons at Cat Crossing Farm

Copyright © 2017 by Judith Stanton
ISBN 978-1-63534-081-5 First Edition
All rights reserved under International and Pan-American Copyright Conventions.
No part of this book may be reproduced in any manner whatsoever without written permission from the publisher, except in the case of brief quotations embodied in critical articles and reviews.

Publisher: Leah Maines

Editor: Christen Kincaid

Cover Art: "Heading for Safety" by Kim Werfel Portraits and Fine Art

Author Photo: Bud Rudesill, photographer

Cover Design: Frogtown Bookmaker

Printed in the USA on acid-free paper.
Order online: www.finishinglinepress.com
    also available on amazon.com

Author inquiries and mail orders:
Finishing Line Press
P. O. Box 1626
Georgetown, Kentucky 40324
U. S. A.

Table of Contents

Snapshots 1
The Three-legged Doe 3
Snow Forecast 4
Perigee Moon 5
Mothers' Daze 6
First Fawn 7
Lone Fawn 9
What the Turtle Knows 10
What the Snail Wants 11
April Aftermath 12
Deer Scat 13
The Lone Fawn Speaks 14
Fawn Tag 15
Summer Morning Drive to Town 16
Twin Fawns 17
Little Brown Bird 18
Flat Out 19
The Critic 20
Back Atcha 21
Country Roads
    1. Curve 22
    2. Ditch 23
    3. Hill 24
Persimmon Tree 25
Fall Falling 27
Pearl 28
Cathedral 30

*With deepest thanks to
Mary Barnard, Ralph Earle and Bonnie Korta
for believing in my wild world
and to Irene (Pony) Gaskin pig midwife
and Ennis Loflin cattle farmer
for telling me I got it right*

Snapshots

i

Which to prefer
the beauty of the leap
the pause
the moment our eyes meet

ii

A buck in velvet
scrapes tree trunks
shreds riffling in the breeze

iii

Antlered bucks in rut
does in heat rear leap
dart cavort for them

iv

Fall winds cut the woods
rusty summer coats
now gray as bark

v

O armed men in camouflage,
don't you know
bucks hang out in gangs
does gather families?

vi

I've seen the mists of England
woven into tapestries
sweat-stained coursers
baying hounds, knights
nocking arrows, drawing
letting go

vii

Hungry deer criss-cross
the frozen pasture
mood grim
glitter blinding

viii

Twenty snow-capped fence posts
at the edge of the deep woods
a lone doe lifts a foreleg, bolts

ix

A ten-point buck leaps the gate
arcs to freedom

The Three-legged Doe

After long drought
the white oak drops
three times as many acorns
as in a year of good rain.
Under its spreading limbs
the three-legged doe stops to gorge,
right front leg sheared off
halfway between her knee
and hoof—victim of a car?
a stump hole in the woods?
or the black rocks in the stream
she crosses to get to my yard?

In the pasture I pick her out
two hundred yards away
shoulder sinking every stride
her stump touches ground
or the lurch when she bolts
with the herd full speed.

At dusk I see her
flanked by last year's twins
and this year's lone fawn
its spots faded by November,
its coat like hers turned gray.
He rams her udder hard.

She watches for hunters
lurking in the woods

Snow Forecast

Record cold this winter,
my hay-fed horses do
not hold their weight.
I give more grain at dawn,
wet fog pressing brown grass
shriveled in the pasture.

On my lawn half a dozen does
forage leftover pecans
acorns spiked with ice.

In the middle paddock
wary bucks hug the far fence
heads heavy with trophies—
a couple of two-pointers
I must have seen as fawns
an eight-point buck
their ten-point leader
heads up scenting the wind.

Weather's changing.

They head for deep woods.

Perigee Moon

Tonight's full moon creeps
up the sky closer to earth
than in nineteen years.

Abroad a tsunami floods Japan.
We launch an assault on Libya,
France and Britain joining in.

At home, deer commandeer
the south pasture
too far away to make out
their particulars.

I grab binoculars
sneak across the yard
peek around the Leyland
cypress's drooping branches
and count, one five eleven
sharpen focus thirteen
sixteen. Four lie in
short spring grass. No,
five, now six, at rest.

Rare to catch them napping
but this winter's been hard
this evening's mild, hunt
season's over, and tonight
the big moon rises.

Mothers' Daze

Pregnant again, the old doe plops
heavy in high spring grass
chews her cud a soft breeze blowing
golden clouds of pollen from the pines.

Nearby her companion grazes
ears flicking flies and ticks
both girls thick-waisted, patient, slow.
The old doe dozes, wakes to find
her friend gone to the far side
of the three-board wooden fence
she leapt last fall with ease.

Not now. Tail flailing, she gathers
as if to jump it, crouches to
test if she can fit under.
                                    Gathers again.
Too clumsy.
               Crouches.
                         Too fat.

Alone she paces the fence
comes back to the rutted track
drops to her knees squeezes beneath
belly scraping the ground
lifts and lumbers for the woods.

First Fawn

I watch for you all spring
fragile in your mother's belly
growing larger stronger
as she galumphs across
the middle pasture
last year's twin fawns
yearlings now, her herd
her core, grazing
safe around her

I watch for her belly
to go flat

I watch for you
at the edges
of the woods

am I early
are you late

I drive out
an evening with friends
take backroads home
at dusk braking
for your sisters
brothers uncles aunts
grazing the shoulders
of Hamlet Chapel
and River Roads

I slow to forty, thirty
can't afford to wreck my car
can't bear ever again
to feel that thud

Light fading
I drive downhill
toward Chicken Bridge
which spans the rocky Haw
the Trout Quintet
on my old car's
old-fashioned radio

and there you are

no bigger than a fox
spots pristine white
legs like fiddlesticks
scrambling up a bank
steeper than stairsteps
into the untamed tangle
of old growth forest

where your mother
waits for you

Lone Fawn

After our gallop my little bay
comes down to a walk
and swishes through
damp fescue scattered
with last year's broomsage,
straw-colored and knee high.

He balks, his back dipping
under me, locks his knees,
lowers his head and pricks
his ears at something
curled up in the grass.

A newborn fawn
flicks an ear
and freezes.

We freeze too,
my little bay and I.

The fawn's spots dot its back
like automatic rifle fire
sparkling in the early light.

What the Turtle Knows

Despite last night's soaking rain
I pull onto the road's soft shoulder
for a turtle making its stately way across,
its domed, mottled carapace dark brown
and gold, pale yellow pollen glowing in
growth rings striated as canyon walls.

They say move them to the side
they're headed for on the theory I suppose
that turtles, too bulky to twist or turn,
travel in straight lines unlike deer
who zig and zag and vault and soar.

Its red eye and flatter dome tell me
he's male and in no hurry—
females' eggs once laid
will wait for him for years.

I pick him up. His head
and splotched legs retract.
His hinged shell snaps shut.
Why did that turtle cross the road?

Not, I think, to get to the other side.
That's not a concept in his atavistic brain.

He crossed because we paved
the prehistoric path his kind
once possessed with full rights
in their noble search for worms and bugs

What the Snail Wants

Little snail, night wanderer,
why cross my driveway
in the middle of the day?
I pick you up, your whorled world
no bigger than a nickel, your slimy
body flesh-colored as my skin.

I turn you over, gravel bits
clinging to your sticky foot.
Crusher run was not a hazard
sixty million years ago when
your kind inched across the earth.

Afraid the bits will hurt you
I push them off. One sticks.
I pry it loose. You squeak
slam down your antennae
retreat inside your shell.

I meant no harm. The daily
FedEx truck could squash you.
With abject apologies from my species
I find a spot of good clean dirt
under dogwood trees
amongst vinca and expiring daffodils
and set you free to roam with deer.

But what if you hoard gravel bits and
squeaked because I stole your treasure?

What if I spoiled your bold adventure
across a vast and daunting plain?

April Aftermath

Saturday afternoon, tornadoes
race across the Piedmont, implode
a big box home improvement store
splinter houses, plow fields
break barns and slaughter horses
rage on to crush three siblings
in their mobile home and a cousin
toddlers huddled in the bathroom.

Overnight the spiky pyracantha
in my driveway puts out
tiny white blossoms that will
yield bitter berries come fall.

Writhing around it,
a parasitic honeysuckle blooms,
its white and yellow trumpets
sweetening the air.

On my way to fetch the morning paper,
I pick a blossom, nip the stem end
and suck its honey nectar,
at one with does who plod up
from the piney woods
bellies thick with promise
to graze bright spring grass
that survived the storm.

Deer Scat

Scat in the rose beds
scat in the drive
under the pine trees
dotting the lawn

down in the ditches
where day lilies grow
scattered on flagstones
that lead to the porch

by the nandina the deer
strip of red berries
over to beauty bushes
and swamp azalea
they prune for us.

Two hundred dollars
worth of tulips
beheaded before
they bloomed.

Whose property do
they think this is?
my exasperated
husband asks.

Ours, their cloven
hoof falls whisper,
since the dawn of time.

The Lone Fawn Speaks

My mother nudges me
from safe green vines
and undergrowth
out to sunshine
clover pasture
tickling grass

I leap
and kick
and bounce
and buck
then oops
she calls
me home

I slip between
fence boards
into brush
and bramble
her rough tongue
sweet breath
warm milk

Fawn Tag

Mid-June,
at the pasture's edge
the trees are all leafed in—
red buds, tulip poplar,
sweet gum, blackjack oak.
The air is clear, dusk golden,
tender fescue ankle high.

Two does watch
three spotted fawns
bounce around on spindly legs
skid to halts, butt heads
launch tiny bodies
in fierce bursts of speed.

You're it.

    I'm not.

        You can't catch me.

Practice practice practice.

Summer Morning Drive to Town

Deer hurtle through
banked pokeberries
shoot across the road

then a flash albino doe
ancient as a pine cone

I brake in breathless wonder

How did she survive
a winter of no snow
her mates' coats
like the bark of trees?

I imagine
the old white stag
last sighted
at the grist mill
could explain
the burdens
of singularity

Till then she'll
fend at the edge
one of the herd
and not one of the herd

Twin Fawns

Two fawns barely old enough
to graze slip inside the fence
from the shelter of the woods
spots still bright
their mother on patrol.

I look away and sigh
at the disorder of
my kitchen—last night's
pasta with Italian sausage
onions and green peppers
took a lot of pots. I ought
to clean up my mess now.

But they're the first twins
I've seen this spring
skinny fluffy fresh
and I look back
only to find them gone.

Any pursuit of wonder
requires obsessive vigilance.

Little Brown Bird
Or gray. It could be gray.

Lands light on a branch
of pussywillow neglected
beside a corner of the house,
then dives into the shrubbery
overrun with white oak seedlings
spreading lemon balm.

It's back in a second, beak
clamped on a squiggly worm
devours it in three swift gulps
and darts off past the walnut tree
toward the setting sun.

What was it? Not a swallow,
robin, cowbird, bluebird,
jay, mockingbird,
my yard familiars.

Mornings, a hermit thrush wakes me
any time I leave the windows open.
Could she be this drab?

Then I think—and it's a stretch—
Brown thrasher! Juvenile.
Smaller than an adult.

But the bird's long gone,
worm dead, craw full,
and I'm still not sure.

Thrasher? Thrush?
Thrush? Thrasher?
I don't know enough.
Never know enough.

Flat Out

August morning, brutal heat
sapped our strength since May.
The horses, in no hurry,
nicker for their brunch
when twenty feet away
a big doe ratchets by,
tail down, stride stride,
leap, stride stride, leap,
her four-month fawn behind
chased by some shepherd mix
its coat tawny as the fawn's.

Who dives into brambles,
safe I think, but then four bleats,
a pause, three more, and silence.

This is my first coyote, new
to Piedmont North Carolina,
more deadly than a lightning strike.

Midday a lone doe at the gate
stares where her fawn split off,
haunted by the lack at her side.

The Critic

Chrr chrr, Squirrel
scolds the tom
who comes too
near her fence
perch, a pecan
in her paws.

Chrr chrr, Squirrel
scolds the crow
who blocks the
board she runs
along then hops
a dipping limb.

Chrr chrr, Squirrel
scolds the doe beneath
the spreading oak.
You let Coyote
kill your fawn.
*Chrr chrr chrr
chrrr chrrr chrrr.*

Back Atcha

Rats on stilts, my neighbor grumbles,
and fingerfires an imaginary gun
at a deer vandalizing his fields,
legs like cornstalks, but moving.

I pay a local farmer to mow
my south pasture, great round bales
rife with broomsage, ceresa lespedeza,
Johnson grass, invasive milkweed.

Horses won't touch the stuff
but he don't care.
It's good enough for cows.

Sorry, I say, about the deer.

Naw, he drawls, props an arm
on the tailgate of his pickup, grins.

He eats my corn all summer,
and I eat him all winter.

Country Roads

1. Curve

Dead of winter
Crawford Dairy Road
I angle my F-150's
rust-and-navy carcass
down a sharp blind curve
marshy bog on either side

A big doe arcs into my headlight
speed flings her into the other lane
and in an instant, terror,
a red truck hurtles toward me
bumps across her broken body
shudders to a stop

I get out, small and shaken
A big black man in overalls
steps out too and offers me
his warm and calloused hand.

You okay, ma'am?

I am.

Can you drive home? he asks so kind.

I can. He climbs into his truck
and I mount mine and we drive off
her leap of death no blood
no mark but memory

2. Ditch

Dinner out in Chapel Hill.
Risotto Milanese. Tiramisu.
Sometimes they let me out,
I joke to my friend.

True. I'm such a hermit. Almost
home on Old Graham Road
I drive through corridors
of pines and oaks on deer alert,

my gaze sweeping the shoulders
as I think about an email
I need to send before I go to bed
when slam up from the ditch

a doe flies into my fender,
a hit so hard my hands rattle
on the steering wheel. I inch
home in my crippled car,
checking my rear-view mirror.
An SUV approaches, slows. Stops.

Morning after, limping to the body shop,
I pass my skid marks
only to find her carcass gone,
fresh meat in someone's freezer,
food for dogs or family.

3. Hill

You aren't a Chatham County-ite
till you kill your first deer
but you can drive for years,
deer on the left, the right,
holding back, bobbing across the road,
missing you by inches till one day
up the road from Chicken Bridge
a twelve-point buck crashes
your front fender and leaps
to his feet, dazed but alive.

Sick, you pull off the road,
helpless as he staggers up the hill
to a fallow field of goldenrod
and Queen Anne's lace
as if he'd be safe among familiar weeds,
as if he could go home.

A ratty pickup rumbles to a stop.
A country boy in jeans stomps out
props his knuckles on his hips.

You want 'im? he asks. *No,* I say.

No way. Hot pangs of sympathy
wash my thighs. The buck crumples
to his knees, skin quivering,
and gasps a final breath.

Country boy whistles admiration
at the big buck's mighty rack.
Cool, he says. *I'm takin' this'n home
'n lying to all my friends.*

Persimmon Tree

Persimmon is a color,
a fruit, a mouth-puckering,
tongue-curling,
face-squinching risk
if you don't know the secret
my horses taught me
and the deer, foxes,
possums and raccoons.

*Don't pick persimmons
off the tree.*

Wait for the first cool nights
of late September, mid-October
better, after they let go
the limbs that spawned them
then splat on the ground so hard
their dusky orange skins burst
and the slippery sweet pulp
not red or orange or yellow
oozes through the cracks
gathering grit from beneath the tree
and fragments of dried leaves
already fallen so close, I had
to learn to look to find them.

If fastidious, you can rinse
the pulp under the frost-free pump
behind the barn. But I urge you
to eat it as it fell, grit
rich dirty minerals and all
the way I learned
from my four-footed friends.

The trick is to beat them to it
stealthy greedy Gusses.

Then if you walk out
midday, attentive, lucky
you can gather a handful
of persimmons warmed
by the autumn sun sweet
and rich on your tongue.

Fall Falling

Persimmons splatter
walnuts plop on soft earth
ping tin roofs like pistols
on a practice range.

Golden leaves or roseate
or rusty brown scuttle
across the pavement
like birds with broken wings.

A buck on the caution yellow
deer-crossing sign leaps
a single bullet hole
piercing its metal heart.

Pearl

At dusk I dig out a frozen pizza
set the oven to preheat
note the deer herd out in force
and hurry to my desk upstairs
when brakes squeal on the road out front.

One of the cats? my nightmare.
I throw on a jacket, shoes,
sprint down three minutes max.

No, not a cat but a doe,
white belly bright against
charcoal gray asphalt. I kneel,
bereft, and touch her ears,
her ribs, her flank still warm,
her coat soft, silken.

So sorry, I say, *sorry, sorry,*
and drag her to the shoulder
her unmarred body smaller
lighter than deer look in the field.

Next to where her body lay,
I see a scrap of flesh
in a pool of blood
ruptured placenta
the tiniest fawn
expelled on impact
eyes closed ears flat
against a seahorse head
perfect pearly cloven hooves.

I cannot leave her in the road.
Her pink wet body fits
my hands like a kitten.
I stumble across the yard
sobbing. She will never stand
on knobby legs learn to leap.

Tomorrow I will dig her grave
under the big white oak.

Cathedral

i

Poplar, oak and cedar poke
steeples in the summer morning
sky. The bee sermon drones late.
Deer spill onto new-mown pasture,
nibbling blades of sweet grass,
gossiping with girlfriends.

ii

In fall the leaves turn amber,
ocher, crimson, ruby, brown,
kaleidoscope of stained glass
swirling in the air. Antlered deacons
sniff the sanctuary incense,
cold damp rising from the stones.

iii

A rare snow, and naked branches
buttress the sky, haven for cardinals,
wrens and sparrows who chirp hymns
of praise, forage under leaves for bugs.
Deer hooves carve frozen paths
like stairsteps worn by sandaled monks.

iv

Snow melts. First fawns push out,
wet bodies baptized at the font
of humus beds. Dogwoods' new leaves
reach up like tiny hands in prayer.
The bird choir molts into new robes,
whistling, warbling *Worship, here.*

Scholar and novelist **Judith Stanton** invites readers into *Deer Diaries*, her first collection of poetry. As a scholar, she edited *The Letters of Charlotte Smith*, a definitive edition that helped restore Smith's reputation as the first Romantic poet and has garnered Stanton the 2017 Distinguished Aluma Award at the University of North Carolina at Chapel Hill. A romantic herself, Stanton published four historical romance novels, *Wild Indigo* and *His Stolen Bride* with HarperCollins and *The Mad Marquis* and *The Kissing Gate* with Leisure Books and Montlake Press. Recently she published her first equestrian suspense, *A Stallion to Die For,* with her own Cat Crossing Press.

Stanton gets much of her inspiration from her farm. Several years ago, on again seeing the three-legged doe grazing under the massive white oak outside her study, she wrote a poem about that doe's courage, releasing her decades-long closet poet to find a new voice and a new mission—documenting the lives of the deer she sees every day on her farm, birds, squirrels, and a very special turtle and snail.

Deer Diaries has been for Stanton what authors call a gift book. From the moment she wrote "The Three-Legged Doe," deer she'd watched for decades consorted with her to show her more of their daily lives from comic moments to tragic ones, stock and staple of lives lived wild. Stanton was privileged to have the time, place, and freedom to learn their quirks, humor, resilience, and courage.

Friends who've read *Deer Diaries* tell her without fail that now when they drive their county roads, with deer liable to dart out at any moment, they drive more carefully.

May you drive more carefully on your roads too.

www.ingramcontent.com/pod-product-compliance
Lightning Source LLC
LaVergne TN
LVHW041506070426
835507LV00012B/1363